NIKSEN
The Power Of Doing Nothing

Tess Jansen

NIKSEN

The Power Of Doing NOTHING

Everything you need to know about Niksen

Tess Jansen

ISBN: 978-8225649877

© 2020 by Tess Jansen

All rights reserved.

No part of this publication may be reproduced, distributed, or transmitted in any form by any means, including photocopying, recording, or other electronic or mechanical methods, without the prior written permission of the author, except in the case of brief quotations embodied in critical reviews and certain other commercial uses permitted by copyright law.

Table of Contents

Table of Contents 5
Foreword 6
What exactly is Niksen? 8
Niksen and Hygge 15
How can Niksen benefit my life? 28
My Niksen Journal 34

Foreword

A horrible 2020 is nearly behind us.

Optimistic as I am by my nature, I believe a great and bright future lies before us.

Among all the recent turmoil and uncertainty that seems intent on continuing into the 20s, it can be nice to take a minute to focus on some of the more pleasant trends of the last ten years, many of which, conveniently, have specialized in acquainting us with new ways to de-stress and work towards finding a moment or two of serenity in our increasingly worrisome world and hectic personal and professional lives.

In the second half of the 2010s, two major wellness trends of Norther European origin – the Danish *hygge* and the Swedish *lagom* – poured over into the popular cultures of English-speaking countries, promising us new ways to learn to take life more slowly, to enjoy the little things, to stop and smell the proverbial flowers: an antidote, their proponents assure us, to the many ills of our still-young millennium. As the Latin saying goes: *omne trium perfectum* (every set of three is complete); and now a new trend named 'Niksen,' recently imported from the Netherlands, seems poised to bookend a sort of Northern European trilogy of early century wellness lifestyles.

What exactly is Niksen?

In the original Dutch, Niksen is a verb derived from the pronoun *niks*, which means, simply, 'nothing.' Etymologically, it's essentially the same as our own word 'nix.' To *Niksen*, then, basically means: to do nothing. To do nothing! To do *nothing?* Nothing at all! Hard sell for a lifestyle, some might say: how can you make a wellness trend – or *any* trend, for that matter – out of *nothing?* The answer, of course, is that it's not that simple… and yet, at the same time, it sort of is.

In her 2018 book "Deviced! Balancing Life and Technology in a Digital World," psychologist Doreen Dodgen-Magee explains Niksen as being like having the motor running in your car while keeping it idle. Others have simply called it "doing nothing with a purpose." That purpose, of course, is to recharge your proverbial batteries, to take a moment away from your responsibilities to both calm your body and clear your mind. Easier said than done, for some. Many who try it out for the first time have trouble allowing themselves the apparent luxury of idleness. *Lekker Niksen!* (sweet Niksen) the Dutch may call it, but in countries like Britain and the United States it can sometimes smack of laziness – something our work-oriented cultures, traditionally, have little patience or understanding for. As a result, the average Anglophone trying his or her hand at Niksen for the first time might feel a sense of guilt and embarrassment, which ends up, of course, having the opposite of the intended effect. Training yourself to allow for these Niksen moments can, because of this, feel a bit like learning a new task – in other words, it takes practice! It could be said that the word itself, the very fact that we're relying on a neologism rather than simply calling it "doing nothing," masks our hidden desire and very real need to allow ourselves those little moments of idleness. As Brittany Wong put it in her 2019 article for HuffPost: "Americans have an uncomfortable relationship with taking it easy" and "that's exactly why we need a little Niksen in our lives. […] It's not being lazy if you call it Niksen."

In other words, finding a trendy new term for something that should maybe seem like common sense can be a way to free us from negative stereotypes, from harmful taboos that have been deeply imbedded into our collective subconscious.

Once you've allowed yourself to let go of the stigma associated with inactivity and accepted the value of doing nothing, the next difficulty that often arises when attempting to strive after that *"lekker Niksen"* is the inconvenient fact that the mind, when you don't give it something specific to work through, tends to wander where you wouldn't necessarily like it to: you think about your worries, you remember all the tasks you've left unfinished, both professionally and in your personal life. As a result, your daydreaming turns sour and ends up causing more problems than it solves.

A study published in 2013, intitled "Pros and Cons of a Wandering Mind," warned that some research participants trying to engage in purposeful daydreaming found themselves getting "caught up in ruminations" which ended up affecting them physically: they experienced increased heart rates for up to 24 hours after the experiment and had trouble falling asleep at night – hardly what you'd want from a wellness lifestyle! On the other hand, the same study suggests that, when you do it right – the researchers suggest focusing on pleasant daydreams about family and friends – there will be long term benefits for your emotional wellbeing, and you will increase your enjoyment of life.

If you're still having a little trouble getting started, try to free your mind by first distracting your body thanks to little things you can tinker with without too much effort or purpose. The Niksen queen herself suggests Baoding balls, kinetic sand or gravitrams, though presumably the recently ubiquitous fad that was (and still is?) fidget spinners could be another alternative. When you're ready to just sit still and do nothing *physically* but are having trouble with *mentally* distracting yourself, you might find a useful (if somewhat basic, and perhaps a little silly) image of the sun setting over a calm sea for two minutes. If you so much as move your mouse, it will reset the timer and invite you to try again. "Just relax" entices a subtle caption etched across the golden light glistening through the few, thin clouds that gently embrace the dying sun, "and listen to the waves." The image itself doesn't provide any audio; but imagining the sound of the waves sloshing soothingly across the water in the warm summer evening, serenaded by the gentle cries of a few circling gulls, is ostensibly part of the exercise.

Once you have more familiarity with just letting your thoughts go, you can begin to find time for it in your daily life. It might help to deliberately pen it into your schedule, but that's not essential: once you've trained your mind to do it, you'll find there are actually quite a few cracks in your daily routines that you can likely squeeze a little *lekker Niksen* into. When you wake up to start your day, while sipping your preferred morning beverage, try taking a moment to clear your mind and do nothing. Just enjoy the warmth of your mug in your hands, the delicate dance of the vapor emerging from it, and think of nothing in particular. If you commute to and from work on public transportation or carpools, try looking out the window on the train, bus or car (when you're not on driving duty!): just let the sights pass you by like a screensaver, let the sun wash over your face or the rain glisten across the window. If you pick your kids up from school, try to get there a little early and just sit in or against your car and daydream for a bit. Of course, it's also something to consider doing right when you're in the thick of it: at the height of your stress, when you've hit a wall at work, for instance, and just can't think anymore, forcing yourself to go on won't get you anywhere, and obsessing over your lack of productivity can just eat into your time even further. Instead, try sitting back for a few minutes, clearing your mind, and treating yourself to a taste of that *lekker Niksen*.

Other examples might come to mind once you get in the habit of trying to find them, and of course the best way to do it will differ from person to person. That's part of the beauty of it: there is no special technique you need to learn in order to practice Niksen, you just need to take the time to do it and learn to let it happen in your own way. The goal is to regularly cultivate these little moments that belong to you and only you, that don't really need to serve any specific purpose other than just letting it all go for a little while and allowing yourself to simply *be*.

The goal is to regularly cultivate these little moments that belong to you and only you, that don't really need to serve any specific purpose other than just letting it all go for a little while and allowing yourself to simply be.

Niksen and Hygge

Since Niksen apparently comes to us as the third in a kind of trinity of lifestyle trends, it might be helpful, in order to better comprehend and cultivate it, to understand a little more about Hygge: the wellness practice that started it all.

The Danish-imported concept of *hygge* (pronounced hoo-guh or hue-ga) made its debut in the Anglosphere's collective imagination around 2016 with a series of how-to books promoting the traditionally Scandinavian lifestyle. "Danes,", "are aware of the decoupling between wealth and wellbeing. After our basic needs are met, more money doesn't lead to more happiness and, instead, Danes are good at focusing on what brings them a better quality of life." Hard to argue with that: who couldn't honestly do with some better quality of life? Great. So, how does one *hygge*, then?

First off – what *is* Hygge? Ask anyone for a definition and you will invariably be told that there is no exact translation into English. If we struggle to define the term in our own language, though, it seems a few other languages do have quivalents: *gezelligheid* in Dutch, *Gemütlichkeit* in German, *mysig* in Swedish and *mattari* in Japanese. Norwegian even seems to have two, with the same *hygge* existing in their tongue alongside the more nationally exclusive *koselig*. Since most of these words are found in our sister Germanic languages, one might ask: why does English appear to be the odd one out in having no native translation of its own? It seems that, yet again, our work ethic doesn't traditionally allow for something so quaint – and, for some detractors, whimsical – as Hygge. And it's precisely this "stiff upper lip" approach to life that the new cultural import seeks to change.

The description we generally get of Hygge is usually expressed with words such as "cosiness," "comfort," "relaxation" and so on. Signe Johansen, author of "How to Hygge: The Nordic Secrets to a Happy Life," at one point equates it to "healthy hedonism." The epitome of this concept might arguably be found in the recipe for Scandinavian mulled wine included in her book.

The best way to grasp the term could be to describe the feeling one gets when experiencing it, and how to obtain that feeling. Mulled wine is one way, but there are many others which are perhaps more familiar in English-speaking countries like Britain and the United States.

1. Lighting candles

Candlelight is quintessentially *hygge*. It's warm, primal, and kind of gathers you into a cosy little bubble of light rather than flooding the room with it. If you light a few candles in the evening or on a dreary winter day, a kind of calmness comes over you, and time might even seem to slow or stand still. A good way to de-stress while maybe listening to relaxing music, sipping some herbal tea and immersing yourself in a good book. If you have access to a fireplace, even better – better still if it's a "real" one, as opposed to electric or gas: the smells and crackling sounds of the wood are key to setting the mood. If you can't get yourself near a fireplace, and the candles are too expensive, try turning off the overhead lighting and illuminating the room instead with a few aptly placed lamps that use non-fluorescent lightbulbs.

2. Pastries

Tebirkes are what the Danes themselves might recommend, though any pastry will likely do. Cookies should be acceptable, as well. Bonus points if you've baked them yourself – cooking can be a kind of leisurely labour, a way to take your mind off things by physically doing something productive without *feeling* like you're doing something physical *or* productive. Enjoying the fruits of your own handiwork afterwards with friends is like the icing on the cake.

3. Sweaters

Well, warm clothing in general, really. Especially if it's hand-knit. Caps, socks, mittens, you name it. There's just something about being snug in the rustic fanciness of personalised woollen garments that makes you feel safe and cosy!

4. Warm company

You can see a pattern emerging here: warmth in cold times. Seeing as how the trend is of Scandinavian extraction, it's not difficult to fathom why. If outside it's snowy, cold, far below zero Celsius for much of the year, you can either live in denial and melancholically await the return of summer or you can learn to live with – and even, ideally, love – the weather you have. Britain and certain parts of North America might not have such extreme cold as countries like Denmark and Norway but making do with bad weather of different sorts is an almost universal human need. And, as in virtually all things, the warmth of good camaraderie can make even the worst of days into the very best of memories.

Other prescriptive books and articles will recommend different variations on the sensation and how to cultivate it, some of which don't involve being indoors or even cold weather at all. Some examples out there include cycling to work, taking an early lunch, and not staying at the office longer than you're obliged to. The general recurring principle, then, seems to be a deliberate cultivation of emotional wellbeing by taking life slow and enjoying it in little bites rather than large, excessive mouthfuls that could lead to a sort of indigestion. In other words, and moving away from the culinary metaphors: great orgiastic moments of joy – large parties, binge drinking et al. – might deliver a greater, more ecstatic pleasure, but such moments are usually expensive, increasingly rare as we advance in our age and careers; and when we can manage to secure a steady stream of these moments, they tend to burn us out quite quickly, leaving us more often than not in a bad way. And if that's the only way we know how to enjoy ourselves, the moments in which we all, at some point or other, find ourselves without that kind of fun and excitement (unless, I suppose, you're fortunate enough to be insanely rich and famous) can seem all the more dreary and dull. By learning to take life one moment at a time, to find pleasure in the little things, we can teach ourselves to feel more satisfied, fulfilled, and validated in a more regular and sustainable way.

By learning to take life one moment at a time, to find pleasure in the little things, we can teach ourselves to feel more satisfied, fulfilled, and validated in a more regular and sustainable way.

It's not hard to sense that Hygge and Niksen are somehow related. Both are about living life more slowly, about finding value in activities that aren't what we might usually consider "productive." There are, of course, some obvious differences: while Niksen emphasises doing *nothing*, Hygge is more about doing *something* – whether an activity *per se* or simply the act of setting up a certain atmosphere – that doesn't *feel* like you're doing something.

So, there's a bit of an opposition between the terms as well; though that doesn't mean they can't still be complimentary. For starters, practicing Hygge can initiate you into the general gist of these trends: it can get you acquainted with the feeling of not being *obliged* to be constantly doing something while still keeping you somewhat occupied. As such, it's more socially acceptable in our culture, which also makes it easier to start off with. The fact that it has a deliberate social aspect to it could also encourage your friends and co-workers to join in on the trend, thus expanding the circle of people you know who are open to experimenting with these new ways to de-stress. That way, once you do get around to trying Niksen, you'll already have a group of people who support (rather than misunderstand, if not outright judge) you as you try to overcome the initial awkwardness and guilt of avoiding all activity.

Hygge might also help with the problem of getting "caught up in ruminations" when you're still getting used to clearing your mind. If your thoughts keep jumping back to stressful things as soon as you try to clear them, it's likely because they've mostly been occupied with stressful things. It seems reasonable then to assume that if you make your activities more *hygge*, your mind should then have more peaceful sensations to meander to when you're chasing after that *lekker Niksen*.

There's a bit of overlap between the two concepts, as well. Imagine, if you will, that you're with a group of friends sitting around a cosy fire, enjoying hot cocoa on a cold winter's day, reading together or playing relaxing card or table games. Maybe someone is cooking something in the kitchen and the smell of biscuits drifts aromatically into the living room where the bulk of you are gathered. Maybe some gentle coffee-shop music is humming along in the background; maybe the snow can be seen softly falling to the ground outside, through the frost-glazed window, as the air turns blue for the lateness of the hour. If even for a fleeting moment, in the midst of all this, your mind drifts away from the group and becomes blankly fixed upon the crackling flames, if you are filled with a warm glowing feeling to match the visual scene before you but your thoughts are briefly distracted from the material goings-on, from the activities themselves, however pleasurable they may be, and from the people and sounds you've surrounded yourself with, retaining thus only the sensation of wellbeing that they bring you, to better cultivate and nourish it all so as to cherish it later when you'll need it most… well, dear reader, would that not be both Hygge and Niksen?

How can Niksen benefit my life?

Still worried these trends might be a little too outlandish to be practical, if not too downright whimsical to find a place in your actual daily life? It's true that they can come as a bit of a culture shock to the average Britton or American, for whom the idea of constantly keeping busy is so deeply embedded in the collective subconscious that some academics have begun to notice how busyness has come to replace leisure as a symbol of status and wealth. After all, our most common word to describe pretty much every conceivable economic activity is "business" which, etymologically, essentially, *means* "busyness."

At the opposite extreme, Scandinavian countries are regularly experimenting with new ways to reduce the average citizen's burden in acquiring the basic necessities of life, with Finland having recently unveiled a plan to limit the work week to a mere four days. *Four days!* Contrast that to the traditional American meritocratic mindset which demands that absolutely everything must be earned through hard work, to the extent that when activists and politicians so much as speak of something like state-funded healthcare for all – a public service which has been ubiquitous in neighboring Canada, cousins Australia and New Zealand, as well as all across Europe for a few generations now – they tend to be accused of leftist radicalism. Even the generally progressive New York magazine once lamented, in an article about Hygge: "What many Americans do not aspire to is Scandinavia's high taxes or socialist ideas. When transferred to the United States, the kind of understated luxury that the Danes consider a shared national trait starts to seem like little more than a symbol of economic status," insisting that like "many of the best things from Scandinavia, *hygge* [and, presumably, *lekker Niksen* as well] might seem, to some Americans, to come with a whiff of smugness."

Still, you shouldn't have to be a radical leftist to see the appeal in taking things a little easier. Or, more concretely: you don't need to "feel the Bern" to feel the effects of *burn-out*, a recently identified syndrome of excessive stress at work which the World Health Organisation has just last May recognized as a serious global health concern. Even when on vacation, the double-edged sword of modern communication technologies (smartphones, laptops et cetera) can keep us from truly disconnecting and enjoying our free time. In 2018, the American Psychological Association published a survey warning that 28% of adult Americans end up working more than they expected to while on vacation, with 21% reporting significant levels of stress during these supposedly relaxing getaways. The worst part, perhaps, is that this tendency to work when we're supposed to be taking it easy has been shown to negatively impact our personal relationships, as well. In other words, even when you finally *do* manage to get away from all your work and its many related responsibilities, the time you're actually able to spend entirely dedicated to your spouses, friends and other loved ones is going to be more stressful and less of the solace and relief that we generally expect from that time. Harsh.

Little wonder, then, that stress is on the rise. In their 2019 report, the Gallup Global Emotions Report, a world-wide survey conducted every year since 2005, placed the U.S. in 39th place out of 143 countries in terms of freedom from stress, while Britain came in 46th place. According to the poll, 55%

of Americans reported feeling stressed out "a lot of the day" against just 35% for the worldwide average. This ranks the United States as comparable, as far as stress is concerned, to some other countries more commonly associated with deep social unrest, such as the Philippines (where 58% said they felt a lot of stress) and Tanzania (where 57% percent answered likewise).

OK, fair enough, you might say: so, we could all go for a little less stress. Great. Still, you may be asking yourself: why Niksen, specifically? After all, there are a myriad other lifestyle trends out there which promise to lead us to a more enjoyable and stress-free life. We've already taken a look at Hygge, which, it turns out, is quite complementary with Niksen, but there are many, many more: from yoga and meditation to specialized diets promising to free you of harmful toxins, or simply to make you leaner, fitter, and thus, presumably, happier; with many exercise routines promising similar results. So, how is Niksen better than any of these options?

Well, "better" is perhaps not the most useful term to be using here. All these techniques are valid and helpful, and of course, being each of us distinct individuals, we'll all have our own preferred method to let go of our troubles. What helps one person to better deal with their stress might be a little less effective on another. Still, compared to all the other options out there, Niksen presents itself as being the most flexible, the most universally applicable. Think about it: diets require enormous dedication, and, usually, special foods which tend to be more expensive than the average nutrition. Exercise routines usually require a personal coach and/or a gym membership. Yoga requires training, usually with a professional (at least, if you really want to get the most out of it). Each of these methods cost money that we don't all necessarily have or want to spend this way. Many of them will also take big chunks of time out of your schedule, which, coupled with the commute to and from the places where you practice them, can be a source of stress in and of itself. With Niksen, though, you don't need any of that. All you need is to do is take a deep breath, clear your mind, and enjoy doing nothing for a few minutes. You can do it at work, you can do it at home, you can do it pretty much anywhere, even while you're travelling to your local gym or weekly yoga class.

So, whether you need a minute to refocus at work or want to make the most of your other activities, don't be afraid to treat yourself now and then to a sweet taste of that *lekker Niksen*.

My Niksen Journal

www.ingramcontent.com/pod-product-compliance
Lightning Source LLC
LaVergne TN
LVHW041642070526
838199LV00053B/3511